Caring for Kittens

Beginners Guide on
How to look after a kitten

by Elizabeth James

Contents

Legal Notice:

This book advocates caring for kittens gently and calmly, training them, not punishing them, and feeding them good food.

Chapter 1:

Choosing a Kitten: How To Choose The Personality That's Right For You

All kittens are cute. But they grow into cats and become all different shapes and sizes with personalities that can greatly differ from their soft furry early days as a kitten.

Kittens need to be totally weaned from their mothers when you adopt one. This helps them learn to develop their socialization skills.

If you take a kitten away from its mother before that you will have problems. Unless it's a rescue life and death situation, it's better to wait. If you hear about a cat who has just given birth, you can claim a kitten and visit, but do not take it until it is ready.

Ideally you want to choose a kitten from a litter that is still with the mother. This is so you can see how the kitten interacts with his or her siblings.

You will get a better idea of the kitten's personality this way. You will find out if its timid, aggressive, friendly or nervous while it interacts with its brothers and sisters.

You can decide if it's a personality that will work with you and your family. If the kittens parents are social and human friendly chances are the kitten will grow into a kitten that is human friendly with the proper socialization from the mother.

If the kitten senses fear from the mother when dealing with people chances are the kitten will react the same way.

How a kitten is handled from birth has a lot to do with how it grows and interacts with others.

Kittens who are handled throughout the day by people and are exposed to many people from the ages of 2 weeks to 9 weeks tend to be friendlier and adjust to humans better and even other animals too.

By the same token, kittens that did not have a lot of contact with humans or were handled roughly or mistreated may grow timid, fearful or aggressive.

The best scenario would be a kitten who was born in a home with a family. This way, sounds in the home, like telephones, TVs and different noises don't scare the kitten as easily as one who was not exposed to them early.

The 2 to 8 week age period is also good for them to get used to the sounds in a home as well.

Look at how the kitten interacts with its litter. Does it play with its brothers and sisters. Is it a bully, is it timid? All these considerations later will help determine the kittens personality.

You do not want to pick a kitten that is too aggressive. Likewise kittens who hiss and hide when you approach them will be difficult to train into people friendly cats as they grow.

You also don't want a kitten to cower or show fear if you try to pet it. Healthy well adjusted kittens want to play with you. If you take a string with you and pull it out and drag it to see if the kitten responds. Kittens love to play and if it's not willing to play there is a behavior problem and that may not be the best choice.

Kittens that were not reared by their mothers or with the siblings may grow up with more behavioral issues than those that stayed with their family.

As a kitten in a cat family they learn modes of appropriate behavior by interacting with the mother and each other. For example they are taught that biting and scratching is not acceptable when they are in a litter. If they are hand reared they are more prone to displaying that type of behavior.

A kitten that approaches you first is most likely the dominant one in the litter. On the plus side this is the confident and adaptable kitten.

On the down side this one may grow into a independent bossy cat that likes to rule the roost and any other pets you may have.

Shy kittens have to be raised very gently. Most likely they will always be sensitive. These kind aren't the best with children or other pets.

Each Kitten has their own traits that make them unique that stay with them their entire lives. By eight weeks a kittens age of development is like that of a two year old child.

Chapter 2:

Choosing a Kitten - Domestic or Pedigree

Another issue determining personality of a kitten is type of breed. Most kittens that people get are mixed breeds called a domestic cat. It can be a domestic long-haired, a domestic short-haired etc.

Domestic kittens are usually a result of a random mating of two cats. Neither of the cats heritages are known. The majority of cats in North America are Domestic Cats.

Many times you can acquire a domestic kitten or cat from neighbors, human associations including shelters, want ads and pet stores. The average price for a mixed breed domestic kitten runs about $50.00.

They have different colors and patterns with varying hair lengths. Each one's personality is as unique as their looks. One of the best things about getting a mixed breed kitten is often you are saving its life. Every year millions of these kittens are put down because no one wants them.

Pure Bred or pedigree kittens are those whose parentage is known and is controlled and documented. This kitten's parentage meets a written standard to describe what the ideal of the breed is and what it should look like.
With pure bred kittens their personalities are generally predictable. Pure Bred kittens are a rare commodity making up 3 to 5 percent of the cat population on this continent. There are nearly 40 breeds that are recognized in feline registry organizations in North America.

A pure bred kitten will grow up to represent the breed both in looks and personality. Many times a person may want a particular breed for either looks or personality or both.

Here is a Guide Chart of Common Pedigree Cat Breeds:

Breed	Hair	Characteristics	Personality
Abyssinian	Short Hair	Ticked coat; ruddy, red, blue and fawn colors	Busy, active, agenda-driven and affectionate
American BobTail	Longhaired and Shorthaired	Medium to large, naturally occurring, bobtailed cat	Loving and intelligent
American Curl	Shorthaired and Longhaired	Ears curl back, away from the face; available in a variety of colors and patterns	Energetic and affectionate
American Shorthaired	Shorthair	Stocky, working breed: available in a wide variety of colors and patterns	Even tempered and quiet
American WireHair	Short hair	Crimped, springy coat; available in a variety of colors and patterns	Even temperament
Balinese	Longhaired	LH variety of Siamese; chocolate, seal, blue and lilac point colors	Vocal, affectionate, active
Birman	Longhaired	Stocky body with white feet	Sweet and

		and point color pattern; easy to groom coat of intermediate length	affectionate
Bombay	Shorthaired	Glossy, black coat	Playful and affectionate; lap cats
British Shorthaired	Shorthaired	Stocky, sturdy, plush coat; blue is very popular but also come in other colors	Calm and quiet; enjoy people
Burmese	Shorthaired	Stocky and well muscled; sable, also champagne, blue and platinum	People oriented, affectionate
Chartreux	Shorthaired	Blue only, well muscled, medium woolly coat	quickly become attached to their family
Colorpoint Shorthaired	Shorthaired	Non-traditional point colors	Vocal, affectionate, active; can be insistent
Cornish Rex	Shorthaired	Soft, wavy, curly coat; many colors and patterns	Active, racy, affectionate
Devon Rex	Shorthaired	Naturally curly, wavy coat; many colors and patterns	Pixie look and personality
Egyptian Mau	Shorthaired	Spotted pattern in silver, bronze and black smoke	Athletic and active
European Burmese	Shorthaired	Moderate type with gently rounded contours	Highly intelligent, affectionate and extremely loyal

Exotic	Short haired	Body and head type like a Persian but with a short plush coat; available in same colors and patterns as the Persian	Sweet, affectionate, quiet
Havana Brown	Shorthaired	Chocolate brown	Busy, affectionate
Japanese Bobtail	Longhaired and Shorthaired	Short pom-pom tail; many colors and patterns available	Active, intelligent, and affectionate
Javanese	Longhaired	Longhair variety of the Colorpoint Shorthair	Vocal, affectionate, active; can be insistent
Korat	Shorthaired	Thai "good luck" cat; silver blue coat and a heart shaped face; muscular	Energetic and affectionate
LaPerm	Longhaired and Shorthaired	Medium sized, curly coated; many colors and patterns	affectionate, gentle and while very active, enjoy sitting in a comfortable lap
Maine Coon	Longhaired	Large, rugged cat; many colors and patterns are available	heavy cat; many colors and patterns are available Quiet and gentle
Manx	Longhaired and Shorthaired	Tailless cat from the Isle of Man; thick, dense coat; heavy cat; many colors and patterns are available	Quiet and gentle

Norwegian Forest Cat	Longhaired	Stocky and hardy with a heavy coat	Active and sweet
OciCat	Shorthaired	Spotted hybrid; athletic and muscular	Strong, active and social
Oriental	Longhaired and Shorthaired	Siamese style cat without the point markings; over 150 colors and patterns are possible	Vocal, affectionate, active; can be insistent
Persian including Himalayan	Longhaired	Stocky body, long full coat, round head with a short nose; broad face; available in a variety of colors and patterns	Sweet, affectionate, quiet
Ragamuffin	Longhaired	Large size, large expressive eyes, all colors except pointed	Docile, people loving and affectionate
RagDoll	Longhaired	Large cat with color at the points	Docile, placid and affectionate
Russian Blue	Shorthaired	Short, dense silver tipped blue coat	Graceful, playful and quiet
Scottish Fold	Longhaired and Shorthaired	Ears folded forward and down; large round eyes; also available with straight ears; many colors and patterns are bred	Affectionate and laid back; sweet expressions
Selkirk Rex	Longhaired and	Naturally curly coat; rounded, stocky body	Quiet

Shorthaired

Siamese	Shorthaired	Long, slender body with typical color at the points - chocolate, seal, blue and lilac; long slender legs; long wedge shaped head	Vocal, affectionate, active; can be insistent
Siberian	Longhaired	Russian native breed; rare outside of Europe	Large and powerful
Singapura	Shorthaired	Warm beige, ticked coat; large expressive eyes; small cat	Sweet, demanding, affectionate and occasionally bossy
Somali	Longhaired	Longhaired variety of the Abyssinian and available in the same colors	Busy, active, agenda-driven and affectionate
Sphynx	Shorthaired	The "hairless" cat; rare	Active, affectionate
Tonkinese	Shorthaired	Originally developed from Burmese and Siamese; strikes a balance between the two parent breeds	Can be vocal, people oriented
Turkish Angora	Longhaired	Originated in Turkey; silky intermediate length coat; long body; several colors and patterns	Busy, curious
Turkish Van	Longhaired	All white except for color on head and tail.	Sweet and interested; enjoy water

Chapter 3:
Assessing The Health of A Kitten

You want to make sure the kitten you pick is healthy before you bring him or her home. There are certain signs to tell that you are choosing a healthy kitten. Even when you choose a kitten that appears healthy you want to take it to a vet to make sure.

First, check their coats. It should be smooth and soft to the touch. The coat should not be dry to the point of dandruff. You want to make sure there are no bald patches or spots. That is an indication of ring worm. You want to make sure there is no evidence of parasites as in lice and fleas.

Flea dirt looks like tiny black-red granules which dissolve into red on a moist paper towel. Fleas look like big brown spots on the kittens skin. They also leave behind black spots. Constant scratching is a sign of parasites on the skin. Beware if you get a kitten from a farm. Often these kittens will have fleas, lice or ringworm. In this case it requires an immediate trip to a vet who can give the kitten the proper medicine and treatment to get rid of these pests. You don't want to bring a kitten into your home with fleas, lice or ringworm. It can get into the furniture and infest another pet.

Look at the eyes of the kitten. They should be clear with no tearing or discharge. A kitten's eyes should be dry. The eye should open fully. The third eye lid should not be visible. If it is then it is a sign that the kitten is ill or has eye damage.

You want to make sure the vision is good by either having the kitten follow your finger as you move it in front of them or take a string with you and let the kitten follow the string with its eyes.

You can also check the kitten's eyes by covering one of the kittens eyes and then move your other finger slowly to the uncovered eye. The kitten should blink. Repeat with the other eye.

Next look at the nose. It should be a clean nose with no nasal discharge. A kittens nose should not be too dry however. It should have a velvety feel to it and be slightly moist. They should not sneeze or have trouble breathing either. The kitten's breaths should be steady and even. If the breathing sounds strange or labored it can be an indication of an infection.

The ears need to be clean and odorless. There should be no head shaking or scratching. A black granular discharge or dark colored wax can indicate ear mites. The ears should be dry and relatively wax free. I f kitten is scratching his ears repeatedly it may be a sign of a problem.

Open the mouth to check the gums.

You open their mouths firmly but gently. Do not squeeze. Their gums should be pale pink. Healthy gums are a sign of a healthy kitten. Their tiny teeth should be white and in alignment. They should not have any bad breath or odor from their mouths. You want to make sure their mouths have no sores or ulcers as well.

You want to check the anal area as well. On rare occasions kittens are born without anal holes. This is life threatening.

The anal area should be clean with no discoloration.
If the kittens rear is dirty it may be a sign of diarrhea or an allergy the kitten has. Diarrhea is dangerous to kittens because they can dehydrate very quickly. Also any discoloration or matted fur can be evidence of parasites as well. In a kitten tape worms on the anus may look like cucumber seeds.

The kittens body should look symmetrical. And they should not look too thin or have a protruding belly which is a sign of intestinal parasites. The kittens belly should look round but not engorged. The kitten should have no lumps or bumps on his or her body. Including at the umbilicus or belly button.

The kitten should display good coordination and no head tremors. Some cats are born with extra toes but that does not create health issues for them.

When checking for the health of a cat please keep in mind that some breeds have distinct characteristics that may not look normal to us but is normal for the breed. For example the hairless breed of cats that look strange and wrinkled. Some breeds appear thin but that's their characteristics. Domestic bob cats are tail-less for example.

You want to check for the sex of the kitten. Males are generally more aggressive than females. Unless you are a breeder yourself, you want to make sure you take your new kitten to the vet to make sure it is healthy and find out when you can neuter or spade the kitten if you wish to.

Depending on where you get the kitten it may or may not need its first shots.

If you see a kitten that has health issues and still want to adopt it, then the vet is a must for you to find out what you are up against in caring for a cat with health problems.

They will also tell you how costly it will be taking care of a cat of that nature. It doesn't mean that it won't make a loving pet but may require care that you may or may not be able to handle.
If at a pet shop you have your eye on a kitten but are not sure that it is as healthy as you would like it to be, then you can ask them if you can take it to the vet before you decide to purchase it.

They may agree. The end result is that you want to check your new kitten with a vet to make sure that you are getting a healthy little one and if it does have a problem and you catch it in time you can avoid a sick kitten with a costly bill.

Chapter 4:

Making Your Home Safe For Your New Kitten

So, now it's time to bring your new kitten. You need to make sure that you house is kitten proofed first. Just like a baby, kittens try out new things which means they get into everything.

Their favorite thing to play with may not be the toy mouse you purchased. Instead you may find that they much prefer chords from blinds, electric chords and wires and plants (that may prove toxic).

Also beware they like to claw furniture and curtains. Things like tinsel from Christmas tree decorations, rubber bands, buttons, beads, needles, and safety pins can choke a kitten or a cat and like a child have to be put out of their reach.

Likewise, small pieces of a toy that can come off or even bells can all pose a hazard. This goes for small sharp objects like twists on a bag can perforate a kitten or a cat's intestines, which could prove fatal.

Your new kitten is like having a baby or small child so dangerous cleaning chemicals, pesticides, antifreeze, and other dangerous chemicals need to be out of kitten's reach.

You may have to put safety locks on cupboards that are in the kitten's reach because they can learn how to pull them open.

Always keep your washing machine and dryer doors closed, and check carefully before and after each use to make sure your kitty hasn't somehow climbed inside. For some reason, all kittens seem to love exploring underneath the refrigerator - make sure that they cannot get all the way under or behind the refrigerator. Fill up those spaces or put boards or other material there to keep the kitten out.

Cover outlets adequately with tapes or plastic conduit electrical cords because kittens and cats like to chew and gnaw through items.

Watch for lightweight table lamps that can fall over, heavy irons that can fall off ironing boards etc.

Look out for reclining chairs where kittens and cats can get up inside and suffocate or get trapped and badly injure or kill themselves if someone unknowingly sits down when they are inside.

Things with loops like shopping bag handles both paper and plastic are potentially dangerous for kittens as they are for babies.

In addition, any plants that may be harmful to kittens, such as those listed below, should be kept out of reach.

Here is a list of plants that are poisonous to kittens:

    1. Bulbs (includes Amaryllis, Hyacinth, and especially Lily of the Valley)
    2. Lupine or Bluebonnet

3. Rhubarb

4. Azalea, Rhododendron

5. Tobacco

6. Buckeye or Horsechestnut

7. Spurges or Euphorbia (this includes the common ground cover, Snow on the Mountain)

8. Black or Bitter Nightshade, Climbing Bittersweet, Horse nettle

9. Milkweed

Soil can also be a source of parasites for kittens as well, so any non toxic plants also need to be out of kitten's reach.

There are more complete lists of toxic and non toxic plants for kittens and cats available online if you Google them or you can ask your local pet shop for a book that has them.

In the , make sure all the medicines are locked up. Shut the bathroom door when you run water in a bathtub. Make sure your toilet seat lid is always closed.

Windows should be completely screened particularly if you are high up. Also make sure that the screens are secure because they will lean on screens and put their body weight on it if they take a nap. If you have a fireplace make sure it is tightly screened. If you have a laundry room or garage keep the door closed.

Secure garbage because it may contain things that can hurt your kitten like sharp openings of cans that can cut their mouths and paws. If you have mouse traps keep them out of sight and reach of the kitten.

It is suggested by many kitten and cat experts that you actually get down on the floor to look around from a kittens perspective. Anything that is dangerous that you can spot from that perspective needs to be secured or removed.

If you can see it and get to it so can a kitten or cat.

Chapter 5:

Things You Need For Your New Kitten's Arrival

Once you finish kitten proofing you can now bring your new kitten home. As a suggestion, you can make sure you have these items in place before you arrive.

Kitten Food - Kittens need more fats and proteins than adult cats. There are many kitten foods available on the market today.

You want the label for the Kittens food to say "Complete and Balanced Nutrition" and "AAFCO" which means animal feeding tested statement " For All Stages".

Kitten foods are specially formulated for kittens. They will have specific words like "highly digestible, nutrient-dense and uniquely designed to meet kittens nutritional requirements".

Kittens can handle dry food at 8 weeks although canned is better for them. You can keep a little dry food in between the can feeds available for them.

It is highly recommended to give the kitten the brand that he was eating before you take him or her home. You can introduce other brands later, but to start with get the same food and flavour they are used to.

Kittens need to eat 3 to 4 times a day. A kitten should have his or her own feeding bowl. Water should be in a separate bowl for your kitten and available all the time.

Kittens and Cats should be encouraged to drink as much water as they like. It helps keep their kidneys and urinary tract flushed. This helps reduce the potential risk of kidney and urinary tract infections that they can sometimes pick up.

Ceramic non lead glazed and stainless steel bowls are the choice materials. Plastic is not recommended because it can harbor bacteria.

You need to have a litter box in place ready for the kitten's arrival. Put it in a place like the bathroom or where there is privacy for the kitten. Yes cats like their bathroom privacy believe it or not!

It is recommended as soon as kitten comes home introduce him or her to the box. Put them in it a few times and let them wander in the area. Chances are the kitten is already litter trained when you bring him or her home so they adapt almost instantly to the litter box.

Also do not put their food near their litter box. They do not like to eat in the same place they go to the bathroom.

The litter box needs to be kept as clean as possible. They also do not like to use dirty boxes and may urinate or defecate outside of it if it's not clean to their liking. Cats for the most part are very clean animals. Also dirty boxes breed bacteria, which the kitten or cat gets on his or her paws and will track through your home. This can also cause infections because the bacteria can spread from the box to your cat.

This is a common cause for urinary tract infections. There are different types of litter available on the market.

Most cats prefer the self clumping kind. This type is sandy in texture and is easier to clean than the regular clay litter because it clumps into a mass when it is wet and then it scoops up in one piece.

Don't use silica gel litter pearls as it can irritate eyes and lungs etc. and is toxic when eaten. Cats dislike them apparently anyway!

Even the littlest of kittens like to scratch and claw so instead of it being on your furniture, you should have a scratching post ready for your new kitten to use.

When cats scratch it is a way of them marking their territory as well as a way for them to remove old claw sheaths. Most cats prefer a tall vertical scratching post that they can stretch up on. There are many types to choose from some of the more popular ones are made with sisal, rope, wood, carpet, and cardboard.

All local pet stores and the ones online carry a variety of scratching posts to choose from. It is also recommended that you cut the nail a little as well; we will discuss that later in the grooming chapter.

You need to have some toys for kitten when they arrive. Kittens love to play. There are many to choose from. The "fishing pole, dangling lure" kind of toy is a big favorite for interactive play. Just make sure it is sturdy enough that small kittens won't tear off feathers from the dangling part.

Catnip mice are a favorite.

Kitty houses and climbing posts can be simple cardboard creations, to custom built "cat furniture" combinations running into several hundred dollars.

Avoid toys that have sharp edges or parts that your kitten might swallow. Choose soft toys that bounce (the bouncier, the better)

Beware of yarn and toys with strings, as yarn and string are dangerous if ingested; supervise all play with these toys.

Once you have all these things in place it's time for you to go get your kitten and bring them home.

Chapter 6:

Finally Kitten is Home

Depending on various factors in your home, this will determine how you integrate your kitten when he first arrives home. If you have no other pets then it is relatively easy.

The first thing that may occur is that your new kitten may miss her previous family as well as his or her mother and siblings. The kitten may cry for them...if this happens pick the kitten up and comfort them.

Pet them gently and talk to them. You can also put a ticking clock where the kitten sleeps because it will remind them of their mothers heart beat. You can also wrap a hot water bottle in a towel (should be between 100 and 102 degrees F) near by the kitten and it will feel like the siblings to them.

If your home is large you may want to confine them to the place where they eat, the litter box and where they sleep so they can get used to their surroundings. At least for the first day or two. After the kitten feels comfortable and relaxed in your home you can let him or her explore.

If you have other family members you want to gradually introduce them to the new kitten. If you have small children you sit them down first and explain what is permitted and not to be done to a kitten. They need to understand it's not a toy and it shouldn't be chased, hurt in any way, bothered, including when it eats, when it uses the

litter box or sleeps.
Show them how to hold and pet the kitten. The right way to hold a kitten is lace one hand under your kitten's chest and use your other hand to support the rear. Gently lift the kitten into the crook of your arm.

Make sure they understand not to pull the tail, the ears or tease the kitten. Children should have supervised times with the kitten especially when their friends come to play.

Don't be surprised if your new kitten or cat hides for the first few days you bring them home. If they came from a shelter or a pet shop they are used to smaller spaces so they hide because it's a new environment. As they adjust they will come out more and become comfortable.

Spend as much time with your new kitten to bond with it. The more time you spend the faster and stronger the bond becomes. If kitten doesn't want to be picked up then pet him or her and introduce a toy and play with them. It's a process, as they warm up to you they will become more affectionate and feel secure with you.

The desirable age to adopt a kitten is between 8 and 12 weeks for socialization purposes. After 12 weeks it is more difficult to socialize a kitten. The first 12 weeks of a kitten's life lays the foundation for their socialization with both people and other animals.

Play time for kittens is very important for their behavioral development. When they stalk and pounce it aids in their neural and muscular development.

It's not a good idea to use hands, fingers, feet or clothing when playing with a kitten, as your cute little kitten will eventually grow into a healthy-sized cat and you do not want to encourage aggressive behavior.

Providing appropriate toys for exercising their natural predatory instincts of pouncing, stalking and chasing will ensure she has a safe and healthy outlet for these behaviors.

Do not use toys that are too heavy for the kitten to move or that are small enough to be swallowed.

Likewise the more petting and handling you give a kitten the more socialized and responsive it becomes as an adult cat. Exposing kitten to as many people helps rid them of fear of strangers as they get older. aAlso those that are not socialized with children reject them or may even bite them when they get older.

There is a technique called Gentling a Kitten. It is a good way to bond with your kitten.

Here are the steps:

·   Gently pick up your kitten at least once a day and speak soothingly to him in a soft, quiet voice. Hold the kitten for 5 minutes or so before setting him down in a favorite spot.

·   After a few days, gradually sit down while holding the kitten. Talk to him quietly and pet him gently. Don't encourage rough play (scratching, biting). If he tries it, tell him firmly, "No." and gently put him down.

·   When kitty is comfortable with the first two steps, stroll around the room holding him and talking to him. Don't distract him with outside elements; he should be focused on you.

·   Put the kitten on a well-lighted table and stroke him. You can talk baby-talk to him if you want!

·   Next day, on the table, pick up a paw and press gently to extend the nails, examine the nails and toes, then gently examine the foot and leg. Get to know the normal feel of his limbs.

·   Back to the table again. This time, examine the kitten's ears visually. You may have to move his head about so you can see inside his ears. Feel the outside of the ears to familiarize yourself with them.

·   On the table again, gently palpitate (press gently) the kitten's abdomen. Stroke his back and sides, feeling for any abnormalities. Again, you're familiarizing yourself with his normal characteristics.

·   Open the kitten's mouth and look at the teeth. Rub your finger along the length of the teeth starting at the gum. Insert your index finger in the corner of his mouth to view the back teeth.

·   By now, your kitten should be totally comfortable with your handling of him, so grooming, teeth cleaning and toenail clipping should be simple. Give him a little treat for being such a good kitten!

These steps should take about five minutes per session doing one session per day, adding more as needed, depending on the kitten's tolerance for handling.

As with all other forms of training, don't make it real chore for the kitten. When kitty gets tired leave it for that day and just pet him. Try again tomorrow.

Inspect your kitten once a week as it grows up.

If you already have a pet there is a trick you can do to make it easier before you even bring your new kitten home. You take a small hand towel and rub it over your current pet. When you go to take your new kitten home you put the towel with them so they can smell the current pet. When you get home you get another towel and rub the new baby down with it and give it to the current pet of the home to smell the new kitten.

You do not put the new kitten in the same room with the current pet when you come home. You confine them to a safe space first that they can adjust to. Give the current pet the towel that smells like the new kitten. This way they will be less aggressive when they meet them because they are familiar with the smell already.
Make their first introduction short and sweet. Remove the kitten after a few minutes. Then re-introduce them adding a little more time.

It takes about a week for the two to get used to each other.

If the two have trouble adjusting to one another keep their time together supervised. Introducing a new kitten to an older pet can be traumatic or stressful for the older one. Make sure you lavish time on the older pet and do not make a fuss with the kitten when with the older one so they do not feel threatened by the new comer.

Make sure if you have other pets particularly cats that the new comer is healthy and has its shots and is de-wormed. You don't want it to spread parasites and diseases to your cats you already have and vice versa.

Kittens that have come from shelters can often have upper respiratory infections and if the kitten is feral check it with a vet first before letting it amount your other pets. They could have ear mites, fleas, or be infected with various viruses.

Chapter 7:

Feral Kittens and Cats

There is a whole world of Feral Kittens and Cats out there. Feral basically means homeless cats and kittens, born in the wild; as well as those that were abandoned or have become lost.

They look cute and cuddly but they are wild animals in a nut-shell. Many of the adult feral cats may have orginally been owned and then cast out or abandoned for countless reasons.

These types and those feral cats that are quiet in temperament with patience can be tamed and brought inside. It is fortunate for those few who can because for the most part feral cats have miserable short lives. It is a gift to change the lives of these sad stray kittens and cats if given the opportunity.

A feral mother cat that is pregnant will give birth in a quiet hiding spot for her kittens safety. Under these conditions the kittens have no human contact and are totally wild.

Usually by the time they can play and romp they wonder into the view of human eyes. These kittens are not easy to capture. If you spot a family of these type of cats they do have traps that you can capture them with from organizations like the Feral Cat Coalition. If you are just taking the kittens its best to do so between the ages of 4 and 6 weeks. You have a better chance of domesticating them.

You can also take an older kitten but the training process is harder and takes longer with less success at times. It depends on the kitten's temperament.

Lost or abandoned domestic cats teach their kittens to be feral. Their latent instincts which go back to their African Wildcat Ancestors help them survive in the open environment. They are like most wild animals. They will not attack unless provoked. But they will defend themselves when they feel cornered or attacked. They will bite and scratch. This is why you never catch a feral kitten or cat with your bare hands or exposed skin.

There are three classes of feral cats. They are classified to help you know how to approach these animals for domestication possibilities.

Class One
These are your true feral cats and kittens. They have been born in the wild. The kittens are second generation to a feral mother. Cats and kittens in this class are terrified of humans. They generally run when they see one. If a person gets too close to this type of cat they will hiss, growl and go into attack mode if cornered. They will scratch or bite so you have to be careful as they may be diseased. Even cats and kittens in this category can be domesticated but it takes a lot of time and patience.

Class Two
These are cats or kittens that were recently abandoned by their owners. They live on the streets. Class two cats and kittens will run from a person at first but not too far. They are very scared. Any sound sends them jumping. If you

feed them regularly they are easy to get close to. As they get used to you they will run to meet you when you feed them and may even rub on your legs. These are the easiest of the feral classes to domesticate.

Class Three
These cats and kittens are so abused by their owners they flee and run away. This is the saddest of all the classes because they are extremely frightened and terrified of humans but cannot survive on their own. They are often rejected from established feral colonies. Depending on the level of abuse inflicted on them will determine their level of socialization and domestication possibilities. The more abused the harder it is for them to ever trust a human.

These cats and kittens are rarely visible to the human eye. They come out late at night to forage for food and run at the slightest sound.

The average life span of a feral cat is less than two years on the streets if it has no help. If they are lucky enough to be part of a colony or there is a care giver to feed them and see that they get spayed and neutered then they can live to 5 years.

It is not good to take a wild kitten from its mother under four weeks. The kitten should be weaned first. Kittens that are taken younger than 4 weeks are vulnerable to diseases and many times do not survive. If you capture the mother with the kittens, the mother should be spayed to prevent her from having future kittens.

It normally takes 2 to 6 weeks to tame a wild kitten. It can take much longer if the kitten is very skittish or is older or is very wild. Even within a litter, kittens will have different temperaments and train differently. You have to be totally committed and patient to tame a feral kitten.
But if you do you saved a little life!

The first thing is when you capture a feral kitten or even a cat you want to take it to the vet immediately. So if you had your eye on a feral kitten, you can make arrangements beforehand. If you can get a sample of the fecal matter to take with you that is good to test for worms by the vet. They will check for flees, lice and ear mites. The kitty will also be tested for Aids and Leukemia as well as other abnormalities.

Here are the basic steps involved in taming a feral kitten:

1. Containment
You need a large pet carrier or cage
Remember the kitten sees you as a threat. Sometimes they are so scared they literally go into shock. If you use a feral cat trap (you can ask your local vet or humane association where to get one) you put food in a bowl in the trap to lure your kitten or kittens and mother. When inside, with thickly gloved hands and with long sleeves and jeans you can transfer the kitten to a sturdy carrier or cage. Immediately remember this is a wild animal. You need to go to a vet to check its health status. They should be tested for contagious diseases before you bring them in your home. Wash your hands between

handling them and wear something like a smock over your clothes. If you can't cover your clothes then change them when you go to your regular pets so as not to bring anything to them.

Once checked out you can keep them in a cage or carrier that is large enough to put a small litter box in as well as food and a water bowl. Do not touch the kitten, cat or litter. For the next three to four days visit the kitten often. Sit next to the cage or carrier and talk to the kitten. The cage or carrier should be in a quiet location and speak softly to the kitten. This helps calm the kitten down. Also for bedding you can use a piece of cloth that you can rub on yourself to give it to the kitten with your scent.

2. Periodic and brief handling with a protective towel

After two or three days you can try to handle the kitten using a towel. Gently place a towel over the kitten and pick it up using the towel. If the kitten stays calm you can gently pet his head from behind. Start with one finger to stroke the kitten when she is eating. When she is less scared you can increase the amount of fingers until you use the whole hand. Never approach the kitten from the front. A hand coming at them will frighten them. This can cause them to hiss or bite. If the kitten remains calm you can grab him like his mother would by the nape of his neck, put the towel in your lap and set him on the towel. You can stroke his body and speak softly to him. Then put the kitten back. The first contact should remain brief. Next contact repeat but have a spoon with a little food on it for it. This wins over many a feral kitten and sometimes even cats.

3. Handling - You can brush the kitten with a soft pet brush. It mimics the feeling of the mother grooming the kitten and the kitten then transfers that need to you. If the vet missed the fleas get a flea comb or flea solution from the vet. It is imperative that you rid the kitten of fleas. Kittens can become anemic from flea infestation and prey to illness. Thi s also helps with the bonding process. Never stare at the kitten too long they take it as a sign of aggression. You can also introduce a toy to the kitten when he gets used to the brushing.

4. Containment in a small room - (this is the second step #2 containment) Normally within 5 to 7 days a feral kitten or cat starts to get past the terror stage and starts to bond with you. No two kittens are the same, so keep in mind some bond quickly and some are shy. The main consideration is that you and the kitten start to build trust between one another. This is done by now letting kitten out of the cage. You can do this within a small space, like a small kitten proofed room, where the kitten can feel free to move around in.

5. Exposure to other humans
As soon as kitten stops hissing and spitting at you, you can start to expose him or her to other humans. Ferals tend to bond with one human which is fine if you plan to keep the kitten. If you plan to adopt the kitten out then do it slowly one person at a time. Do

not have a crowd or you will undo all the behavior socialization that you accomplished.

6. Keep kitten or adopt to a home

Do your research before you give the kitten to their new family. It is suggested to always ask for a donation because it makes the kitten have more worth. Many people will take kittens and sell them to labs. For feral adoptions it is better to have a calm, secure atmosphere with no small children. It's better to place two kittens together as indoor kittens only.

Chapter 8:

Grooming Kitty

Kittens start early on grooming themselves. Their mothers spend many hours a day grooming and caring for her kittens.

Grooming your kitten is a way for you to help bond with it. It doesn't have to be a difficult interaction. It should be enjoyable for kitten and become part of their regular regimen. Cats spend 10% of their day grooming themselves.

The best way to approach grooming with your kitten is to be relaxed. You want to start off with 5 to 10 minute sessions depending on kittens tolerance levels. As kitten gets used to it you can increase the time.

The first step in developing a grooming routine for your kitten is brushing and combing. Brushing and combing helps to reduce shedding and fur balls. When you brush and comb the kitten it distributes the natural oil throughout the coat which helps to minimize matting and leaves the coat shiny and soft.

The length of the kittens hair determines the amount of brushing it will need. It is recommended that long haired cats get brushed daily to every two days. Short haired cats can be brushed once a week. There are different types of cat brushes with different bristle strength from soft rubber to metal combs. Be careful of sensitive areas like the belly, back of legs and tail.

Do not show the kitten the brush you are going to use. Start by playing with the kitten to relax the kitten first. This helps get the excess energy out of kittens system. You can then proceed to pet kitten. Massage behind the ears and under the chin. A female kitten relaxes when you scratch her back right before her tail. If kitten starts to purr then he or she is relaxed enough to begin grooming. When you move into grooming do it slowly.

Pet kitten slowly and then change to brushing without showing kitten the brush. If kitten starts to get finicky then massage the ears again.

Another good grooming tip for kittens is to groom them as if mimicking a mother cat. Take a barely damp washcloth and wipe them down all over with short little strokes, like their mother would do with her tongue. This keeps the little kitten clean and teaches them how to groom themselves as well. It's recommended to do this after they eat. It also stimulates their bowels.

Kittens need their little faces cleaned especially to prevent the buildup of stuff around their eyes. You can use a soft face cloth or a cotton ball dipped in a little warm water.

You hold your kittens head and gently wipe their face down. You wipe the eyes gently and let the tears build up soften and wipe again. You can check kittens teeth for tartar build up which is rare. If kitten has bad breath it may actually be an indication of another problem.

When it comes to the ears, it's not recommended that you clean them unless you can see they are dirty which is rare.

You can gently clean the outer part of the ear, with a piece of damp cotton gauze. Do not dig into the ear or go in too far as this can cause damage.

As far as trimming the claws go; it's good to start as soon as possible so kitten can get used to it. You should have your vet show you how to correctly cut your kittens nails on their first visit. Its best to get kitten used to you touching his or her paw as well as rubbing it even before you attempt nail cutting. The first few times kitten may pull their paw away or walk away. When this happens let it go until another time.

The more you are able to handle kittens paws the more relaxed they will be when you are ready to cut them. When you are able to hold the paws and squeeze them firmly but not hard to expose the nail then your kitten is ready for you to clip the nails. Basically you are just cutting the sharp claw part of the nail.

You can place the kitten in your lap or have them face away from you or you can get someone else to cut them quickly while you hold the kitten. Do not cut to the quick. The quick is the pink fleshy portion of the nail. You want to leave at least a third of the nail intact when you cut it.

Sometimes kittens and cats may need an occasional bath. There are times when kitten will get so dirty that he or she needs to be bathed. For the kittens first bath you do not emerge him in water. Start by taking a warm damp towel . Next apply shampoo to the towel. Now wrap kitten in the towel with the shampoo part on his back. Don't wrap kitten too tightly keep his head out and let his legs pop out. Rub the kitten with the towel gently and speak to him while you are doing it. You can rub his little face too.

At this point you take the kitten by the sink and turn on the water - if the water is too loud and makes kitty nervous turn down the pressure.

You take kitten in his towel and put him under the water. Keeping the towel on him you bathe him, rubbing him with the towel on. You can start to move the wash cloth up and down on the kitten at this point to get rid of all the soap on him.   Once the soap is all removed turn the water off.

Get a dry towel and then rub him carefully dry. Use a second final towel that is dry and wrap kitty in it including his ears. This will muffle the sounds of a blow dryer which may scare kitten. Turn the dryer on low with low heat. High heat can irritate his skin.

Start at the tail and use a small bristle brush with circular motions to dry the fur. You can also rub the towel to keep kitten in a relaxed mood. While kittens head is covered with a towel you can try and put kitten on its back so you can dry the stomach and back legs. If kitten starts to fret, towel dry the head and put kitten in a warm spot so he can finish drying. Do not use leave in conditioners because they can give kitten an upset stomach when they lick themselves clean. Combs work well on long hair and brushes better on short. These are the basics for grooming a kitten. There are variations of course and because different kittens have different temperaments you may have to adjust or be creative to accommodate your kitten's personality.

Chapter 9:

Kitten Behavior

Although kittens look very cute, they can think for themselves and at times their behavior can become irritating!

The best way to deal with kitten behavior and potential problems is to nip it in the bud before it gets out of hand. The better they are socialized and introduced into your home, the better they will behave and adjust to your rules.

Just like babies have milestones in their development so do kittens as they grow into cats. By nature cats are social creatures. As newborns, their mother and then siblings teach them the ways of feline society. Here are the stages and what to expect from birth to 18 months of a kitten's life.

- Like newborn babies when a kitten is born its activities at birth are sleeping and nursing. A kitten will nurse at the same nipple from its mother because of the scent. They scent mark it so they can get to it time and again. At one to two weeks the kitten crawls and begins to acknowledge who's the mother and who are the siblings.

- When kitten is three weeks old up until about four weeks old they are crawling to walking and pouncing. They now begin to initiate play between their mother and with their siblings. Kitten is taught by his family what is and is not appropriate behavior between him and his siblings and mother. Grooming themselves begins and they can regulate their own body temperature – they don't need to be snuggled up to mum any more. Kittens now start to understand what the litter box is by watching their Mommy.

- By the time they are five to seven weeks old, life is all about playing. They start gentle play and learn how to retract their claws while playing. Chasing, jumping and rolling is no included in kitten's play vocabulary.

- If a kitten is female by the time she is three to six months she can become pregnant. So this is the ideal time to spay your kitten if you wish if she is a female. Social ranking also comes into play between three to six months. Kittens are still playful but not like the earlier months.

- Between nine to eighteen months is kitten teenage years. This is the time kitten will test your last nerve to see what he can get away with. They will test the limits and boundaries set by you the owner. This is also the time to neuter a male kitten.

Kittens communicate with us in different ways to try and get us to understand their needs. For example with other cats they will use their tail, nose, claws etc

Kittens can use scent and claws to claim territory. They use various cat sounds as well to communicate. Try to understand these ways and it will help you deal with their problems.

Just like a child or teenager that will try a parents patience so with a kitten or young cat.

Here are some of the common behavior issues you may or may not experience with your kitten.

Play aggression starts to show at around four months. When you are playing with them and they start to get too rough, y can nip that in the bud. You immediately stop playing and say sharply to them 'NO' looking at them when you say it. This behavior is part of their natural predatory aggression that goes back to their ancestors hunting and killing prey in the wild for food.

Cats are natural predators. They are not vegetarian animals. It's in their instincts to hunt down and kill. You can see this incorporated in their play. They will lay in wait and then pounce on a moving object or even you as you pass by. Their play is an extension of their innate hunting behavioral characteristics. What happens is that in a sterile environment, meaning one without prey to attack they take that hunting aggression out on what is at hand.

A moving foot, a dangling object whatever they can hunt becomes fair game for prey. This is why it is so important for kittens to have things to play with. It helps the kitten release their wild hunting urges. Also if you take the time to play with the kitten he will be less likely to bite and scratch you when you do play together.
The main thing is when kitten starts to display rough playing behavior you want to move him away and say no immediately.

Do not reward this type of behavior. For example, if your kitten pounces on you to get his food then don't give it to him. He has to learn not to do that to you; do not reinforce the behavior by giving him the food.

You do have to let the kitten express his hunting urges and that's what the toys are for.

In this way the cat will express his natural behavioral tendencies and not be prone to aggressive behavior due to being restrained from his natural instincts.

Remember kittens are babies and like to play. So, when you have a kitten that nips your ankles when you chase him and you yell to stop he is not necessarily aware that anything is wrong.

If a male cat is not neutered he will display signs of aggression. They spray the house when not neutered to mark their territory and tend to fight your other cats and pets.

Neutered males make all around better pets for the home.

There are those kittens that display the Alpha cat tendency (the number 1 cat over a group).

These are the kittens that turn into cats that think they rule you. These kittens are natural leaders and refuse to be led. They also use every opportunity to be the one in charge. They like their food when they want it and will let you know it.

They may let you touch them for short periods but only on

their terms. They rebel, demand attention and seem to bully you until they get what they want from you. These are the ones that wake you up any time of night, when they are hungry. They may come and tap you, even bite you on your nose.

There is a time when aggression is maternally driven and that is with a mother cat and her kittens.

Even a normally placid cat may display signs of aggression when it comes to her kittens. When your cat becomes a mother you have to understand her aggression is related to protecting her children. If she perceives anyone including you as a threat to her babies she will react as such.

Its best to leave the mommy cat and her babies alone when she first gives birth and when they are very small.

As they grow and she relaxes again around you she will let you handle both them and her. If she is fine about you handling her kittens then go ahead. Do it very carefully at first as long as they are healthy. Wait until a couple of weeks. Start with 10 minutes at a time with the mother present. This is especially good if you don't want to keep the whole litter so they start to interact with human contact.

The bossy Alpha kitties will do whatever it takes to bully and be the boss. The best way to deal with this type of behavior is to ignore it completely. When he is acting like the King in the doorway for example push past him and go about your business. Do not pet him or acknowledge him until he calms down completely. This is letting him know that his bully tactics will not work with you. If you see he is going to attack get something that rattles very loudly like a jar with coins in it or even a spray bottle and spray him and he will run away.

The behavior of a kitten that feels threatened may appear as aggressive but its actually a defense mechanism to protect the kitten or cat.

There are certain signs to look for when kitten is about to get aggressive.

The tails starts to wag, ears go back, they may actually give you a dirty look, they stop purring, they change body positions, they may give a big sigh or even hiss. If you are petting the kitten he or she may react as if you touched a spot they don't like being petted.

At this point, stop petting them and if they are on your lap put them down.

Sometimes a kitten or cat may distrust a human and this is the reason for the seemingly aggressive behavior.

In this case you would treat them as a feral cat and while they are eating you move a little closer each time until you can touch them gradually. You talk to him and may even hand them a treat to help establish trust between the two of you.

You may try petting this type of kitten or cat on the head

but stop if they show signs of annoyance. With this kind of kitten you also want to try to introduce playing with them so they will start to relax with you.

If you have other pets at home or cats they may fight from time to time. Sometimes rough play mimics fighting. Kittens often engage in rough play. They bite, scratch, nibble, wrestle and tug with their siblings and mother as a form of behavior development as I stated earlier.
Kitten fighting however is a violent act. It can be a result of territory disputes and personality clashes. Signs of fighting and not playing include hissing, arched backs and defensive postures.

If they are small enough you can separate them. If the kittens are larger it is not advisable because they can scratch or bite you when you get in the middle.

Get the spray bottle make very loud noises or yell to try and divert their aggression.

There are medical reasons for aggressive behavior as well. One example of such a condition is Ischemic Encephalopathy. Ischemic Encephalopathy is a parasitic condition that primarily affects young to middle-aged outdoor cats. It is caused by aberrant migration of Cuterebra larvae. This condition causes aggressive behavior and so does Hyperthyroidism which usually occurs in older felines.

Chapter 10:

Inappropriate Behavior

There are times when kitten displays inappropriate behavior such as not using the litter tray.

Its relatively easy to train a kitten to use the litter box most of the time. When they are born and grow they see their mother going to the litter box. If they are put into the box a couple of times they tend to naturally use it from then onwards. Its that simple. Its almost instinctive with a kitten.

But unfortunately there are times when kittens refuse to go in the box.

The first and foremost reason a cat won't use the litter box is that they view it as dirty. Cats are for the most part clean animals and they do not like to use a dirty litter boxes. It is also recommended that if your kitten is not completely litter box trained you do not allow kitten free range to the house. You keep them semi confined until they get the idea of how to use the box properly.

If you see the kitten going into the sit position "to make", you can grab the kitten and put it in the box to prevent an accident. Scolding and punishing kittens and cats does not work particularly. They are not dogs and cannot be trained like dogs. Positive reinforcement and praise is what works with kittens.

When you have to go away for a length of time during the course of the day confine the kitten to one room; at one end have food and water and the other end have a clean litter box.

It is also recommended to keep the cat on a regular feeding schedule so they eliminate waste around the same time daily. It gets them used to using the cat box on a scheduled basis.

As mentioned before, the self clumping litter works the best because you can take the wet clumps out and keep the litter dry.   Cats do not like boxes that smell like urine.

Think of it this way; if your cat urinates or poos on the carpet, its cleaned up immediately. A cat box that is not cleaned daily or even a few times a day is not inviting to a kitten or cat to use in to make in. What would you choose a clean carpet or a box that's cleaned twice a week full of urine spots and fecal matter?

A litter box should be cleaned daily and when the soiled litter is removed it should be replaced with clean litter. You should at least once every two weeks wash the box with water to which a little lemon juice or vinegar can be added to balance the acidity of the urine out.   Do not use ammonia it makes the smell worse.

Keep the litter box in an appropriate location that they can get to easily eg near the back door, in the bathroom etc. Cats do not like to defecate in areas close to where they eat or sleep so do not keep a litter box there. If you have more than one feline in the house it is recommended to have more than one cat box available. Their scent marks a box and some cats won't use a box that has the scent of another cat on it.

Other things you can do with a cat who resists the litter box is to periodically call the kitten or cat to the litter box and scratch the litter. Let kitten see the box is clean. Do this after they eat, after they play and if they are sleeping for a few hours wake them up and call them to the box. They will start to get the idea that the box is clean and its okay to use it. This is especially true for cats who are avoiding the litter box because it is dirty.

They may also associate the cat box with punishment if you were previously yelling at them for not using it or pushing them into a dirty litter box. So always be gentle when training and keep the box clean.

There are kittens that seem hyper. If kitten is excessively nervous, jumpy and fearful, you may want to look into what is causing this behavior in kitten. If its a loud noise or a situation you can control then the kitten has to be desensitized to the stimulus that is causing him or her fear.

First you need to accurately identify the source of the fear. Then you try and prevent exposure to it and reintroduce it on a gradient. For example, a kitten may jump out his or her skin when the phone rings. In this case lower the phone considerably to barely a ring. Test the fear inducing stimulus like the phone at a much lower level with the kitten to see the reaction it has to it when it rings at that lower level. If the kitten tolerates the lower sound you gradually over a period of days increase once a day the level of ring and bring the kitten closer to it. As his or her tolerance increases so can the loudness.

Sometimes kittens and cats suffer from separation anxiety. Cats don't react like dogs when they have this kind of anxiety. They don't howl or destroy the whole house. They may however pee inappropriately and you notice it every time you go away for a while.

This may be a sign of separation anxiety. Some cats are more genetically predisposed to this kind of anxiety. Genetic factors do include emotional sensitivity and a predisposition toward anxiety. Certain oriental breeds of felines, such as Siamese and Burmese, may be more prone to develop separation anxiety than cats with more robust temperaments, like Maine coons.

Environmental factors often involve improper bonding experiences when cats are young. Orphaned kittens, early-weaned kittens, and pet store bought kittens are probably at the greatest risk of developing these stressful condition syndromes. Combine the sensitive personality with inappropriate early lifetime experiences and you have a recipe for disaster of this kind.

Some cues to tell you your kitten is suffering from separation anxiety would be:

Over attachment to you the owner

Following you around the house room to room

Behavior of distress as you are about to leave such as whining, hiding looking sad etc.

Vocalization as you leave; crying, moaning, meowing

as you are out the door you can hear it

Anorexia - the kitten or cat won't eat if you are not there

Inappropriate elimination of waste, making in the wrong place

Excessive and compulsive grooming

Rare but does happen; destructive behavior such as scratching furniture clothing etc.

Greeting you like you are a long lost friend.

You can help this behavior by enriching the cats environment so their alone time isn't so stressful. Make sure they have access to view out the window. Have plenty of toys and catnip lures for them around. Leave the radio and a light on for them.

There are also even a medical causes for this behavior also. If you are at all worried about continued anxiety, then see the help of a vet to check there is nothing physically wrong with your kitten.

Behavior like jumping on counters and furniture that you don't want them to can be controlled with things like a spray bottle handy. There are sprays also available in pet stores to discourage animals from jumping or going on furniture because of the smell. It can also work for scratching too when they are using your rugs and furniture.

This is why its good to have a scratching post for the kitten and getting them used to using it early on as opposed to your rugs or furniture.

When you see them scratching an inappropriate thing and you do have a scratching post say no firmly. Move them to the post and put their paws on it to help them get the idea of where to scratch.

If your kitten is doing things like excessive grooming it is considered compulsive behavior which is sometimes a way for them to defuse some emotional upset they are feeling.

Common signs of compulsive behavior are things like:

Wool sucking or eating

Over-grooming/hair-barbering or hair-pulling

Feline hyperesthesia syndrome or 'rolling skin syndrome'
This is where you see signs such as being annoyed with their tail, twitching their tail, going from loving to scared, staring, persistent meowing, dashing off aimlessly, rippling the skin just above the tail...

Very little is known about this condition, but it is thought to be a result of over-vaccinating, low quality diets, preservatives and chemicals.
You need to rule out other health problems by visiting the vet, then embark on a homemade diet or use very high quality pet food for your cat.

I would recommend speaking to a pet nutritionist to get your cat detoxified, learn what chemicals and toxins in the house they should not come into contact with (keep your house as green and natural as possible!) and on a healthy diet.

Believe it or not, pets can get hypoglycemia the same as humans. This means low blood sugar and is a result of overproduction of insulin in the body, an inadequate diet, too much sugar, excessive exercise etc.

Aggression, moodiness, weakness, dashing around can all be signs of this condition as well. The way to combat this is to have structured meal times 3 to 4 times a day of high quality food. This is a recommended feeding schedule:

Breakfast, lunch, dinner, snack before bed. Homemade food is the best. Snacks can be hard boild egg or scrambled egg, cottage cheese, plain yoghurt, chicken, homemade meatballs etc. Again seek the advice of a pet nutritionist.

There are also homeopathic remedies for behavioral problems and physical problems which you should familiarize yourself with. There are also detoxifying remedies that you should look into as well.

With any worry about the health of your cat, seek professional help from a vet and a pet nutritionist.

There is some kitten behavior like suckling or kneading that continues into adulthood. You can redirect kittens behavior to an object that he can continue this behavior with. You discourage him when he does it to you with a loud no, and introduce an object such as a pillow, piece of material or toy he can do suck or knead.

There are some inappropriate behavioral traits that you can correct yourself if you catch it early enough.

Chapter 11:

Conclusion

Remember no 2 kittens are the same – they are all individuals with different likes and dislikes.

Be consistent in the way you train and look after a kitten. This creates predictability for them and helps them feel secure and calm.

Kittens are very curious creatures and they have to explore as part of their nature. There are times however when you just can't figure out what the kitten is doing or why its doing something repeatedly.

It could be that he is pooping inappropriately and you did everything the books said. Kitten may be just too aggressive and you can't handle it. In cases like this its time for professional intervention before you throw in the towel and give the kitten up.

First and foremost take the kitten or cat to the vet to see if there is a medical reason for the behavior. If the kitten or cat is healthy there are specialists around that could help with training etc. I do recommend you get several books on cats and kittens, as there are basic practises but you may find extra tips and points from other cat owners and professionals.

For those kittens that go through the normal stages of being a kitten, once you learn how to deal with a kitten its actually easy. When you and your kitten bond and trust is established you are on your way to having a loving and great companion for the rest of its life!

Printed in Great Britain
by Amazon